PLATFORM PAPERS

**QUARTERLY ESSAYS ON THE PERFORMING ARTS
FROM CURRENCY HOUSE**

No. 53
November 2017

CURRENCY HOUSE

Platform Papers Partners

Platform Papers Readers' Forum

Readers' responses to our previous essays are posted on our website. Contributions to the conversation (250 to 2000 words) may be emailed to info@currencyhouse. org.au. The Editor welcomes opinion and criticism in the interest of healthy debate but reserves the right to monitor where necessary.

Platform Papers, quarterly essays on the performing arts, is published every February, May, August and November and is available through bookshops, by subscription and on line in paper or electronic version. For details see our website at www.currencyhouse.org.au.

THE JOBBING ACTOR:

Rules of
engagement

||||||||||||||||||||||||||||||||||||||||||||||||||||||||||||||||||||||||||||||

LEX MARINOS

ABOUT THE AUTHOR

LEX MARINOS was born in Wagga Wagga, NSW into a family of Greek cafe owners. After moving to Sydney he enrolled in the new School of Drama at the University of NSW and after graduation in 1970 involved himself in Sydney's New Wave. He quickly became a regular in TV comedy on ABC and SBS and also attended the master classes of the visiting American acting teacher, Stella Adler, an experience that had a lasting influence upon his work. Since then he has worked in all areas of the entertainment industry as an actor, director, writer, broadcaster and teacher.

As an actor he appeared with the then newly established companies Nimrod Street, Australian Performing Group, Melbourne Theatre Company, Sydney Theatre Company, Company B Belvoir, Big hART, and at many arts festivals, as well as commercial productions such as *The King and I*. Best known on television for his role as Bruno in *Kingswood Country* (1980–84) and Manolis in *The Slap* (2011), he has also had continuing roles in *City West, Embassy, S.C.O.O.P, Live and Sweaty, Ballzup, World Series Debating; Strictly Dancing*, and *Late Night Legends*. Films include *Cathy's Child, Goodbye Paradise, Last Days of Chez Nous, Bedevil, Backyard Ashes* and numerous short films.

Lex is also well known as a radio presenter, first on 2JJ and then on diverse ABC, FM and commercial networks.

As a director he has worked in all media, notably the film *An Indecent Obsession*, television series *Bodyline, Embassy, A Country Practice,* plus documentaries. He co-founded the King O'Malley Theatre Company and has directed many shows for commercial and subsidised companies and festivals. He was Director of Carnivale, NSW's multicultural arts festival, 1996–99. He directed one of the segments of the Sydney 2000 Opening Ceremony, and was Executive Producer, *YEPERENYE* Federation Festival, which took place in Alice Springs as part of Centenary of Federation Celebrations. He has held many advisory and governance positions with arts and cultural organisations including SOCOG, The Australia Council, and Community Broadcasting Foundation. In 1994 he was awarded the OAM for services to the performing arts. Lex is a frequent speaker and writer on arts and cultural diversity; has hosted numerous awards and community functions; and is guest tutor at several theatre and screen colleges.

His book *Blood and Circuses: an irresponsible memoir* was published in 2014 by Allen & Unwin. Proud member of Actors Equity since 1970.

Dedicated to the memory of Philip Parsons (1926-93),
a wonderful teacher who inspired a generation
of students to love and respect the theatre,
from both sides of the footlights.

Acknowledgements

Like anything I attempt, I can't do it without the help of others, and this essay is no exception. Thanks to longtime friend, Katharine Brisbane, for commissioning the essay and then attacking it with intellect and rigour. She edits with a rapier dipped in honey. To John Senczuk, Martin Portus and Julian Meyrick, who provided encouraging and incisive responses; and to all at Currency Press and Currency House who serve our industry tirelessly.

And of course, to my wife, Anne, who does her best to reduce my pomposity and self-aggrandisement to tolerable levels before they are inflicted upon others.

Finally, thanks to all my colleagues, past and present, who have shared their lives and work with me, and have made me want to write about them.

Introduction

'So, it's come to this,' I told myself, as I lay in a gutter in Waterloo covered in rotting tomatoes. 'Where's the dignity?' I groaned out loud. It was a beautiful summer's day and I was working on a web series in which I'd just been supposedly hit by a car while delivering boxes of tomatoes. It was easier for me to lie there while the crew set up the next shot. I was provided with a cushion, shading and water while the crew buzzed around. As I lay there slowly turning into pasta sauce, I reflected upon the vagaries of being a jobbing actor.

I thought of the old gag about the man who shovelled the elephant shit in the circus. When he complained his workmate suggested he get another job. The man was outraged. 'What,' he said, 'and get out of showbiz?' 'Exactly,' I muttered, 'it's nothing to do with dignity. Dignity left the building a long time ago.' Besides, I comforted myself with the knowledge that I certainly wasn't the first actor to be pelted with rotten tomatoes, just the most recent. I was just a link in the chain that stretched back to the dawn of civilisation.

Storytelling and mythologising are universal phenomena common to all cultures, as though they are primal needs, as basic as food and shelter and sex. Indeed, acting is arguably the world's second oldest profession. It's an easy flight of fancy to imagine the tribe gathered around the fire at night, celebrating the success of the day's hunt, or the defeat of a fearsome enemy, the death of a king, the birth of a princess, the greatness of the ancestors, the glory of the gods, the patterns of the stars, the cycle of the seasons, the evolution of a cosmology. The rhythm of the clapsticks, the drone of the hollow log, the development of songs and dances, masks and costumes of pelts and feathers, paintings on the cave wall, figures on pottery, words on papyrus.

How to define the jobbing actor? Not the handful who find fame and fortune and power. The ones that audiences pay to see. I want to write about the vast majority of actors, the ones that struggle to stay employed. The ones for whom acting is, variously, a hobby, a job, a career, a vocation. It calls to you and you're compelled to follow, despite the obstacles, wounds and slaps. You may not make money or find success, but if it's what you need to do more than anything else, then it's what you do. It's what I do, and have done for half a century. I've been blessed. It's enabled me to help raise a family, live in relative comfort, see exotic places, meet amazing people, work with wonderful artists, find friends and lovers. It's the life I'd hoped for, and it's been my way of trying to understand the world.

T.S. Eliot nailed it in *The Love Song of J Alfred Prufrock*:

No! I am not Prince Hamlet, nor was meant to be;
Am an attendant lord, one that will do
To swell a progress, start a scene or two,
Advise the prince; no doubt, an easy tool,

Deferential, glad to be of use,
Politic, cautious, and meticulous;
Full of high sentence, but a bit obtuse;
At times, indeed, almost ridiculous—
Almost, at times, the Fool.

To be an actor, as I came to learn, you must be able to confront constant challenges: emotional, intellectual, vocal, physical, and technological. You need stamina and resilience, pride and humility. You must be professional and accountable, a team player, and it helps to have a sense of humour. Talent is always useful but not mandatory. A good agent and a supportive union are also important. But the one inescapable attribute every actor needs is luck. When I look back over my working life—not something I'm apt to do except on occasions such as this—the one distinguishing feature is luck. Like a high proportion of jobbing actors, by the time a script hits my desk it usually has plenty of fingerprints on it. I get the job because someone else is unavailable. I accept that and it doesn't bother me at all. My father was a gambler—unfortunately with not much luck— and the one thing I learned from him was that luck exists in the cards you are dealt, or the dice you've rolled. After that it was all about skill, how you played that luck.

1. Finding my way

I grew up in Wagga Wagga, in the 1950s and early 1960s, where my family, migrants from Greece, owned a café. The town had two cinemas and a drive-in. So I saw plenty of movies, but I really liked the travelling shows that came through town. In return for placing their poster in the café window, we were given tickets to the shows: Sorlie's vaudeville tent shows,[1] circuses, concerts, Young Elizabethan Players,[2] amateur musicals and revues. I loved them all. Torch singers, exotic dancers, ventriloquists, rope twirlers, drag acts … the whole kaleidoscope of performing skills and traditions. And, of course, I loved the clowns. I thought that making people laugh must be a really happy thing to do. That was the post-WW2 acting environment in Australia.

When we visited relatives in Sydney, Mum would take us to the Tivoli (on the corner of Hay and Campbell Streets, near Central Station) and the movies, while back home we'd gorge ourselves on television. But for me, radio was the biggest influence. It had everything I was interested in: sport, rock 'n' roll, quiz shows, talent shows, comedies and drama serials. I could dream away hours pretending to be a commentator, disc jockey, quiz master, comedian, a character in one of the dramas.

The family moved to Sydney in the early 1960s. I

completed school and enrolled for an Arts degree at the University of NSW (UNSW). My brother was already fulfilling the family ambition of becoming a doctor, and although I was expected to follow him, I knew that wasn't for me. But I didn't know what was for me. I had become a lonely, insecure adolescent who enjoyed reading, movies and music. I didn't know how to channel these interests, but I thought journalism might be a possibility.

Anyway, as luck would have it, in 1966, I went to the University of New South Wales (UNSW), where the first School of Drama in Australia had just been established. The National Institute of Dramatic Art (NIDA) was already on campus —the first national acting school, set up in 1958–59—and did not welcome the newcomer. A certain rivalry and borderline tension arose between the School and NIDA as territory was disputed between the academic and the practical. Drama had previously been a department within the School of English, to which I gravitated for two reasons: the curriculum piqued my interest with the range of writers to be studied, and there were plenty of girls enrolled. There was a cohort of inspirational teachers: Robert Quentin, Philip Parsons, Victor Emeljanow and Helen Oppenheim. As the School of Drama grew, they were joined by Jean Wilhelm, Marlis Thiersch, William Pollak, John Golder and Oliver Fiala. All of them with specialist knowledge and an infectious love of theatre. I was further influenced by an amazing set of fellow students: directors Aarne Neeme, Rex Cramphorn, Johnny Allen, writer Alex Buzo, actors Arna-Maria Winchester and Gaby Lev (now running her own company in Jerusalem). R.I.P. Rex, Alex, Arna. All of them acquiring academic knowledge to enhance their desire to be professional practitioners.

But I still did not really know what being an actor was: and whether it could be a career.

The School of Drama was my initial training. For the next four years I read every play from Aeschylus to Zola, learned theatre history and drama theory, stole books from the library, took speech and movement classes with some of the NIDA teachers. Even took a course in ballroom dancing at Arthur Murray's dance studio. I can still execute a 'false corner' in a waltz. I appeared in countless student productions, starting with *Saint Joan,* and including Edward Bond's controversial *Saved,*[3] Moliere's *Tartuffe,* Joe Orton's *Crimes of Passion, The Knack* by Anne Jellicoe, and others I vaguely remember. I thrived on the social life, but also enjoyed the acting, and thought it was something I wanted to know more about, something I wanted to do well. Who knows, maybe it could be a career?

And I saw a lot of theatre. At the Old Tote (on campus), Doris Fitton's Independent, Phillip Street revues, the Tivoli revues, J.C. Williamson's musicals in the big commercial theatres, the radical New Theatre (then in Kings Cross). Marian Street in Killara. It was still basically Anglo-centric in style, the emphasis on speech and deportment, proscenium arch style except for the Ensemble, which introduced theatre-in-the-round stage to Sydney.

But there had been changes since WW2 that had impacted upon actors. For a start we were better organised. Actors Equity negotiated basic rates of pay and conditions, as well as being active in Australian content levels, residuals, imported artists etc. The Australian Elizabethan Theatre Trust (AETT) had been established in 1954 to provide government funding for the performing arts and present a better class of entertainment. Not much, but it was a start. Playwriting competitions were held. Australian actors were given scholarships to train abroad and rare opportunities to appear in Australian plays and explore Australian themes in Australian idiom, in plays such as *Summer of the Seventeenth Doll* (1955) by actor Ray Lawler, *The Shifting Heart* (Richard Beynon, 1957), *The One Day of the Year* (Alan Seymour, 1960). Television replaced radio as the dominant popular medium, killing vaudeville as it did so. Movies and musicals still held their own. And there were the beginnings of professional repertory companies: the Union Theatre Repertory Company (now the Melbourne Theatre Company) in 1953; and in Sydney in 1963, the Old Tote Theatre Company. Basically, solid English rep companies doing classics and new work from the UK and America. NIDA had been established to train actors, and American musicals star Hayes Gordon opened the Ensemble Theatre in 1958 to introduce the Strasberg 'Method' to Australia. But there were bigger changes to come.

In 1967, the UNSW Drama Foundation[4] and NIDA converted a church hall in Randwick to support new Australian drama: the Jane Street Theatre. From that time and through the 1970s we saw many new works produced there and at the Old Tote Theatre[5] on campus, under the banner of NIDA. They included *Norm and Ahmed* (1968) by my mild-mannered classmate, Alex Buzo. Suddenly I knew someone who had actually written a play. Writers were not dead or from somewhere else, they were among us, writing about US. *The Legend of King O'Malley* in 1970 became a huge popular success.[6] With similar things happening around the country, a new paradigm was emerging. It was palpable.

Youth culture was demanding its own place in the town square. As Dylan sang, 'There was music in the cafes at night/And revolution in the air ...' The post-war baby boomers had grown up and were changing the landscape and popular culture had to change to accommodate them. We wanted our own movies and records and art. We wanted to be separate from our parents. It was rock 'n' roll, skiffle, folk music, James Dean, Marlon Brando.

The late 1960s have taken on mythological status as a time to be a student. Vietnam, sex, drugs, and rock 'n' roll, decimal currency. I explored them all thoroughly as I grew up in the safe haven of the School of Drama. Two other things influenced me. Though not religious, I loved the ritual of the Greek Orthodox Church and the sense of community it generated. I also loved the atmosphere of the Sydney Cricket Ground (SCG) and the old Sydney Stadium in Rushcutters Bay. It was here I saw Bob Dylan in 1966 and it affected me deeply. It was the height of his controversial conversion to electric music from pure folk. I learned several things that night: art can change people, art can unite people, art is a powerful weapon, and performing art happens in an instant—now it's here, tomorrow it's gone.

Towards the end of my studies I joined an extras agency, to earn some cash and gain some experience. Two jobs stand out. Firstly, a pub scene shot in a bar at the SCG for the classic Australian film, *Wake in Fright* (1971). It proved to be the final film veteran actor Chips Rafferty made, and I felt privileged to be sharing a scene with him, however remotely, and with a couple of hundred others. I felt a link to the earlier years of Australian cinema. Similarly in *King Oedipus* for the Old Tote Theatre Company (1970), directed by Irish director Sir Tyrone Guthrie. This was an elaborate production by one of the grand old men of the theatre; and again I felt a link to the great British theatre tradition. I was among a squad of plague-riddled Theban supernumeraries needed for a groaning, smoky opening scene. Most of them were NIDA students, many of them, including the late John Hargreaves and Wendy Hughes, later enjoyed distinguished careers. By the time I graduated, there was only one thing I aspired to—I wanted to be a jobbing actor.

2. A Time for action

The late 1960s was a time when we could feel the burgeoning sense of national identity, and this was evident in the surge of new writing: Williamson, Buzo, Hibberd, Hewett, Romeril and all. The Government also increased its commitment to national culture. The Australia Council for the Arts was set up in 1968, followed by a host of government film agencies.[7] This activity led in turn to the formation and consolidation of state theatre companies, and the emergence of alternative and fringe theatres. These new companies sprang up in non-conventional spaces —a converted stable (Nimrod) and an old pram factory (Australian Performing Group); and halls, clubs, holes-in-the-wall. They were irreverent and boisterous, political, communal, and defiantly Australian. Like the rest of the world's youth, we wanted to throw rotten tomatoes at the establishment. In Amsterdam, a protest group called Action Tomato was so passionate about ending classicism and discovering new theatrical forms, that they actually did throw rotten tomatoes at classic repertory companies, traumatising the poor bloody actors whose only crime was to be holding down a job. It was a fortunate time for me, since I clearly didn't fit into the older style of British theatre. (Incidentally, there was a time in the mid-1970s when, by taste and circumstance, the directors of all the major state companies were English males.)

I was 21 in 1970, equipped with a strong education, rudimentary acting skills, energy, curiosity and hunger. I joined the union, got an agent, and started hustling. I would give it a go for a year, and if nothing happened I'd look for a real job. I started to get a few small pro-am shows, plus some one-liners on ABC dramas, pantomime for kids at shopping centres. With some friends I started a small staging company where I learnt to build sets, operate lights and sound, and make some money. Back at the School of Drama I did some tutoring. I was optimistic and eager to participate in the great cultural change that was rolling.

My first big break came by taking over a role or two in *Hamlet on Ice* for the Nimrod Theatre Company at their converted stables in Nimrod Street, Kings Cross (now home to the Griffin Theatre Company). Formed in 1970, by John Bell and Ken Horler, Nimrod was at the forefront of the New Wave. A small cramped space, sweltering in summer, freezing in winter, uncomfortable bench seating, a total fire hazard. A unique rhomboid stage with audience visible on both sides, close enough to touch, hear and smell. It was energetic and exciting, and totally new to Sydney. *Hamlet on Ice* was a pantomime by Ron Blair, Michael Boddy and Marcus Cooney, with songs by Graeme Bond and Rory O'Donoghue, and directed by Aarne Neeme in the rough and rambunctious style, which was the hallmark of the early Nimrod. In true panto style, Kate Fitzpatrick played Hamlet and Bob Hornery was Gertrude. I took over the roles of Ophelia (!) and Rosencrantz (or was it Guildenstern?). My first main stage show, it meant a lot to me. I had a foot in the door, and I was able to get a better agent, one with a more prestigious roster of actors, and therefore more likely to be talking to producers and companies. Shortly, another break came my way. Unbeknown to me, the ABC had been looking for presenters for a weekly television magazine show for young people. I met the producers at a small family-and-friends party where we ended up playing charades. Evidently, I did well enough for them to offer me one of the presenter jobs. They also had a commitment to cultural diversity, which was pretty unusual in those days. (As it still is in these days in some areas.)

The regular money was welcome relief but the job also gave me an invaluable opportunity to develop presentation skills and camera technique. I learned how to work with cameras in both a multi-cam studio environment, and on single camera location shoots. I learned how to hit my marks, find my light, wait for the boom to be in position, learn scripts quickly. I also learned about shots sizes and what sort of coverage was needed to edit a story. I became comfortable working in front of the camera.

Next break was an offer from the Melbourne Theatre Company (MTC) to join their Theatre-in-Education company. I was recently married and we moved to Melbourne. The MTC under the formidable John Sumner, was *the* prestige company at the time, and, even though it would only be a schools tour, I leapt at the opportunity to be part of an old-fashioned rep company. Simon Hopkinson and Nick Enright were the writer-directors and we rehearsed a repertoire of four plays. We did two shows a day, five days a week for forty weeks. I also drove the van. We would rock up to a school in the morning, unpack minimal props and sound equipment, do the show in all kinds of rooms, halls and gymnasia, conduct a bit of Q&A. Then, as itinerant actors have always done, we would pack the wagon and head off to the next booking. It was still an era when one could learn on the job, and most mornings we were able to join the major company for vocal and physical classes. Once we accompanied them on a regional tour. We also participated in readings and workshops. I was thrilled to be an apprentice in this system, meeting and learning from my elders.

Under the patronage of Prime Minister Gough Whitlam, the sense of 'Australianness' grew as did the cultural infrastructure and funding. There were regional companies, playwrights' çonferences, a new dedicated niche publisher, Currency Press, began publishing Australian scripts and bringing Australian drama into the school curriculum.

Elsewhere from 1970 other changes were impacting. Led by our union, we marched in the streets óf our capital cities agitating, successfully, under the banner 'Make it Australian', for increased levels of local drama content on commercial television. Government listened and enforced quotas. Production houses, notably Crawford Productions in Melbourne, the leader in Australian TV drama production, began turning out cop shows and comedies. Hundreds of directors, writers and technicians were learning their respective crafts. It became affectionately known as 'Crawford Tech', and one of the bonuses for interstate actors was that a booking for one cop show often meant a booking for a second, thereby amortising the cost of the return air fare. (Three long-running serials were then in production simultaneously: *Homicide, Division 4, Matlock*). The enfeebled film industry miraculously revived, due in good part to the establishment of the Australian Film, Television and Radio School (AFTRS), which opened in 1973, and generous federal tax concessions for film investors. A lot of those movies may have been tax write-offs, but again, they provided increased opportunities for actors, and others, to develop essential skills.

3. Gathering skills

By now it was the mid-1970s and I underwent a few colossal changes. I was married and had become a father. I was getting regular work but needed to keep developing, when along came my next bit of luck. The ABC, God bless her, heard the call of the young and decided to give them their own radio station, 2JJ. Instrumental in establishing it was Ted Robinson, dancer turned radio and television producer, who became a mentor to a generation and a great friend to me. Most of the regular announcing staff were signed up, but there were still the midnight-to-dawn slots that needed to be populated. Ted volunteered to do one of them and invited me (and my Bob Dylan collection) to sit in with him. We had great fun, had a good response and continued to present our show on a weekly basis for the next couple of years.

I had done some radio. ABC radio drama was still being produced prolifically and I'd had a couple of small read-ons, at the microphone in their Darlinghurst studios, standing in awe of the legendary veterans around me: Neva Carr-Glynn, Lyndall Barbour, Nigel Lovell, Alistair Duncan, Don Crosby and others. Voices I had grown up with, sitting by the wireless in Wagga. A link to the golden age of radio. I loved working with them, observing their ability to lift dialogue from the page and tell the story vocally. I also marvelled at their ability to put away several schooners over lunch before heading back to the studio. Other ABC departments, notably Young Persons, also needed voices; but it was Doublejay that really gave me the opportunity to develop my radio skills. Under Ted's generous guidance, I learned how to structure a show, edit tapes and mix effects, sequence music to explore a mood or a theme. I learned how to tell a story through sound. Above all, as with the television series, the work taught me to relax in front of a microphone. I was able to experiment with pitch and pace and dynamics and find my own voice and develop its range. Soon I was being offered other shifts on a flexible basis between acting jobs.

But the most lasting influence on me, in those formative years, was the opportunity to study with legendary American teacher Stella Adler. Born into a theatrical family (her parents ran a Yiddish theatre company in New York)[8] she made her debut aged four or five, transferred to Broadway and joined the ground-breaking socialist Group Theatre where the Strasberg Method was the driving acting philosophy. The Group Theatre was founded in 1931 by the theatre director and critic Harold Clurman, with Cheryl Crawford and Lee Strasberg whose interpretation of the prevailing Stanislavski method of realist performance was to force actors to examine their own emotions and memories as the basis of their characterisation.

Stella disagreed. She defected and went to Paris to study with Stanislavski himself and concluded that imagination was more important for an actor than self-examination. Her view was that Strasberg's method forced the character to become the actor; that this was self-evidently limiting, and that the actor should become the character by exploring the 'given circumstances'—the who, where, why, how and when, events that determine the character.

Stella Adler had been brought to Australia by actress Jone Winchester and the Australian Drama Foundation for a series of master classes. Stella was regal and demanding, a fierce task master, unwilling to accept mediocrity or lack of preparation. 'Don't waste my time', she would growl. I thought my general sense of dramaturgy was pretty good—and it was, from a structural point of view—but she showed me that an actor's dramaturgy was different from that of the writer or the director, and required more forensic skills. She made us dig deeper and deeper into the character's imagined life, building through details, plotting beats and actions, creating the world of the play, revealing the story, looking for new information in every scene, working internally and externally, making choices from the discoveries. In your choices lies your talent, she said repeatedly. It was the greatest growth spurt I ever experienced; and its great value to me was not that I emerged a better actor, but that I felt I was a better actor. I was confident that I now had a process that made sense to me and on which I could rely. It even underpinned the more external, knockabout performing that characterised much of the new writing I was called to perform.

There were also alternative styles to be examined. Non-naturalistic techniques were evident in the alternative Australian theatre of the 1960s and 1970s. In Melbourne the Australian Performing Group (APG) revived vaudeville skills and undertook circus training (Circus Oz developed from this), and in Sydney Nimrod Street was a product of the Jane Street experiment. Two seminal books were studied intensely. British director Peter Brook's *The Empty Space* (1968), and Polish director Jerzy Grotowski's *Towards a Poor Theatre* (1968) had a significant effect on local theatre, notably Rex Cramphorn's Performance Syndicate.[9]

By the time the 1970s came to a close, I had managed to survive my first decade as a jobbing actor. I'd done a few shows at Nimrod Street and had returned to MTC for some main stage productions. I worked in several new venues like the Bondi Pavilion, Nimrod's new theatre in Belvoir Street, Surry Hills, and the Seymour Centre, as well as a show in Hobart's historic Theatre Royal, our oldest surviving theatre. There was even a shambolic drunken production at a theatre restaurant, which soon closed. I had done a couple of films, some television, and quite a bit of radio. I was enjoying the variety of work and thrived on the life of freelancing, not knowing what the next job might be, but confident of something.

The next decade was equally eventful for me, busy with a number of major developments. I fulfilled a couple of acting ambitions: to perform at the Opera House (as the French physician, Dr Caius, in the Sydney Theatre Company's *The Merry Wives of Windsor* directed by Mick Rodger); and to appear in a new play by Dorothy Hewett (*The Fields of Heaven,* 1982 Perth Festival and STC). The Hewett role was that of an Italian migrant, Romeo Bodera, and his love of an Australian girl, played by Natalie Bate in Perth, and Heather Mitchell in Sydney.

Directed by Rodney Fisher, the play examined race and class and isolation in Dorothy's familiar cocktail of passion, politics and poetry.

But more significantly, for my career, I then made the move into directing, as many actors do. It was something in which I had always been interested, and, having worked on so many new plays, I was accustomed to being part of the dramaturgical process. This is one of the distinguishing features and legacies of the 1970s New Wave. The old school of acting kept to a well-worn path and followed the director's interpretation. We were more experimental: there were no dead white males in our repertoire and, more often than not, the writer was in the room. It was more democratic; everyone was encouraged to participate in the process before the director had the final say.

I had also had the benefit of having been at a few Playwrights' Conferences in Canberra. An annual two-week residential workshop begun in 1973, it was always a great gig to win, working intensely on new plays and carousing heavily in between. One of the plays I had worked on (*No Room for Dreamers* by George Hutchinson) was being given a run in a season of new plays by the Ensemble Theatre at the Stables.[10] They were looking for a director and when the writer contacted me I jumped at the chance. It went well and Bob Ellis wanted us to form a company to do more.[11] Bob at that stage owned the Stables, having gloriously bought it to save it from demolition after the Nimrod company moved to Surry Hills. I told Bob it was crazy and it couldn't work unless we had someone who actually knew how to run a company. Fortunately, arts administrator Michael Lynch agreed to join us; and the King O'Malley Theatre Company was formed to present new Australian plays.[12] The sort of plays, as it turned out, that the major companies were no longer doing. By now it was 1980 and the initial wave of nationalism had subsided; the alternative companies had either faded or moved into larger spaces, with bigger budgets and became more risk averse. The youthful experiment was wearing thin; audiences wanted to be comfortable again with known work. We did a couple of successful seasons, the second in collaboration with the Sydney Theatre Company (STC), and then the caravan moved on.

In my case, I landed a television series, *Kingswood Country*, which went on to have several successful seasons (1980–84). It was Australia's equivalent of England's *Till Death Us Do Part* and America's *All in The Family*. Ross Higgins played the racist-sexist-sectarian, dinky-di bigot Ted Bullpitt, the Alf Garnett/Archie Bunker meme. There was a slight hiccup over whether my character, Ted's son-in-law, Bruno, should have an accent, since he was 'ethnic' (in this case Italian-Australian). I maintained that as he was born here he should speak with a normal Australian accent. I was sick of seeing, and playing, stereotypical 'wogs'—not that there were many then in our Anglo-centric television shows. The producers/writers agreed with me, and it proved a smart move, considering the changed social climate that was finally acknowledging Australia's multiculturalism. Many young Australians from diverse cultural backgrounds identified with this character. We did about a hundred episodes over four years, but during the final season I started to extract myself. It was still extremely popular, but I had become restless with the unvarying nature of the work and wanted to move on. It's easy for actors to get stuck with a role that diminishes their flexibility. Some actors also believe that television success stifles their opportunities to work on stage; and the chance to be taken seriously as actors. I don't think it really affected me, one way or the other but I was uncomfortable with being a minor celebrity and its invasion into my personal life. It's understandable that when you are in someone's lounge room every week they regard you as part of the family. It's just that I already had a family and wanted to spend time with them without intrusion. However, it would be churlish of me to complain. I have to acknowledge that there were many advantages. Bruno certainly facilitated lucrative corporate work, and, more satisfyingly, he gave me an easy introduction to a variety of communities.

I was also grateful that the series had come at the right time for me. My personal circumstances had changed: I was divorced and re-married, had inherited a second child, and then had two more. As well as a mortgage and a dog. I obviously needed more income than theatre could provide. Maybe it's my migrant heritage, but I knew that I needed to make good use of the luck and establish some financial security while I could. I had also seen too many actors squander their good fortune, piss it up against the wall, and end up with nothing but a permanent hangover. I picked up some radio work with the ABC, and some presentation work for the newly expanded SBS Television, and mastered the art of autocue, another valuable skill for an actor.

Having directed some theatre and appeared in film and television, it seemed a logical move to direct for film and television. The opportunity came from Kennedy Miller Productions, a new quality-TV production company formed by Byron Kennedy and George Miller. I had been unable to take up an offer to work on *The Dismissal*, their screen interpretation of the dismissal from office of Prime Minister Gough Whitlam in 1975; now they asked me to be one of the directors on their *Bodyline* series (1984), based on the notorious Ashes test series of 1932–33, in which the English resorted to reprehensible bowling tactics to dismiss Australia's invincible batsman, Don Bradman. It was a metaphor for Australia's growing sense of itself and its place within the British Empire. I was also asked to be one of the writers on *Bodyline*, working with an old mate, Denny Lawrence, another actor who had switched to writing and directing. Working with experienced producers, directors and writers was a master class for me, learning how screenplays were structured and written.

After that I received an offer to direct a film, which led to another one and so it went. Working with great cinematographers, editors and technicians taught me how films were shot and made. And I still managed to fit in some occasional theatre, television and radio. I travelled all over Australia and occasionally overseas. For a short time at the end of the decade I was working four gigs a day: editing a film in the morning, co-directing a David Atkins song-and-dance show in the afternoon, directing a small play for downstairs Belvoir in the evening, and finishing off with a midnight radio shift. I needed a break. I had previously experienced a debilitating bout of depression and was desperate to avoid a relapse. I also wanted the kids to have some experience of the world, particularly their Greek relatives and heritage. So I took them to Greece for a year. It was a golden time for us as a family.

4. The Nineties and disillusion

Then came the 1990s and some more unexpected turns. My agent, the wonderful Bill Shanahan, died and I think I lost my way a bit. Bill had been an aspiring actor, who found more satisfying work in administration before realising his true vocation as an agent. He influenced the whole industry and set new standards with his insistence that actors be treated with respect and fair reward. He equally insisted that actors behave professionally and responsibly. He had guided me along the various tangents I had pursued, understood and balanced my needs financially and artistically. I had so totally relied on his advice and direction, and without it I drifted. I had a bit of directing work in television, not much in theatre or film. I toured Australia in the cast of *The King and I* for the Gordon Frost Organisation (a production which was later taken to Broadway, but without the Australian cast) and there was more television, drama and comedy, notably *Live & Sweaty*, a live Friday night sports/variety show hosted by Andrew Denton, that comprised a panel of quasi-commentators to debate the events of the week. The panel regulars were Elle McFeast, Rex 'Moose' Mossop, Peter 'Crackers' Keenan, Debbie 'Skull of Rust' Spillane—and me. I obviously needed a persona, and quickly. Andrew obliged and introduced me as Lex 'the Swine' Marinos, and so I stumbled towards a kind of *commedia* character of an easily-outraged, reactionary stoner. Almost, at times, the Fool. This led to some comedy debates on television, and, more lucratively, on the corporate circuit. And some radio for ABC Sport. I'd always been a big sports fan and being paid to watch footy hardly seemed like work.

I was keen to try and get back into theatre and did a season of short plays at MTC. Much as I enjoyed new plays like *Ned* by Pam Leversha and Andrew Bovell's *Like Whiskey on the Breath of a Drunk You Love*, I didn't feel comfortable. It was all good and earnest, with nice people and great to be acting again, but I'd been away too long. The edge had gone, now it was all about the marketing and the power of the subscribers. It felt unreal, a very bourgeois pursuit.

I had changed too, in what I wanted from the theatre. I was looking for something else, and by good fortune it turned up in the person of Scott Rankin.[13] Scott was putting a show together with some juvenile offenders in Burnie, Tasmania, and was looking for an actor with a bit of a profile who was prepared to work with some troubled youth. He added that they had no money, but was able to offer a bottle of very good Scotch. Of course I accepted, and it's one of the smartest things I've ever done. I enjoyed the challenge, the kids were great and Scott created a beautiful show, *Girl,* relevant and confronting. It was the beginning of an association that has lasted for twenty-five years, and we still enjoy working together.

I became involved in arts politics unintentionally, but

I think I had been gravitating towards it. The White Australia Policy had finally been repealed in 1966 but you wouldn't have known it by looking at our television or our theatre. I was dissatisfied with the lack of opportunity for artists from diverse backgrounds and started to speak out about it. My profile from *Kingswood Country*, and my access to ABC commentators gave me plenty of chances to raise the subject. I was asked to address conferences and write articles. I had de facto become a spokesman for multiculturalism in the arts. Soon I was part of Paul Keating's National Multicultural Advisory Council, the Australia Council, SOCOG's Multicultural Advisory Committee, and others. I also became director for four years of Carnivale (1996-99), a NSW multicultural arts festival. I rapidly developed a new set of skills: writing business plans, budgets, sponsorship proposals, grant applications, policy papers, marketing strategies, and mediation.

To round off the decade and the millennium, I directed a segment for the Opening Ceremony of the 2000 Olympics: a seven-and-a-half-minute story told through dance, music and design, which celebrated Australia's immigration and diversity. We used 750 community performers from all countries represented by the Olympic rings, and choreographed their traditional dance to metamorphose into a united contemporary dance as they were joined by 1,500 young people and the rings and their colours transformed into the outline of Australia.

Like everyone that year, I survived the Y2K virus, and took a gig in Alice Springs organising Yeperenye Dreaming, a large Indigenous festival for the Centenary of Federation. Cultural groups came from all over Australia to perform traditional dances, followed by a contemporary concert involving Indigenous and non-indigenous musicians.

Then I went 'home', where I did some work for Wagga Wagga City Council setting up some events. Interwoven during this time was some irreverent commentary for a dancing show, and writing and presenting commentary for archival sporting programs, which the ABC was digitising. I had also opened up a pleasant little sideline as a stadium announcer at major sporting events. These jobs carried me from the Asian Games in Qatar to a show at Steve Irwin's Australia Park; a documentary in Florida to a festival in Perth. I was working relentlessly and it was taking its toll. I was now in my mid-fifties, on the road too much and I was unhealthy. A year earlier I had been diagnosed with leukaemia; now I had a heart attack.

The leukaemia had been found after my doctor noticed some anomalies in a regulation blood test. He referred me to a haemato-oncologist who announced the bad news. We monitored it for a number of years and I kept working until the fatigue and the disintegrating immunity to common germs started to impair me. It was time to start chemotherapy. Happily, it was successful and, although never cured, it remains in remission.

The heart attack was virtually self-inflicted. I had ignored all the signs—stress, family history, overweight, lack of exercise, smoking, high cholesterol—until the chest pains became insistent. I was on tour in Perth with BighArt, and had resolved to see a doctor just as soon as the show was up and running. But before I could do that

I collapsed in the shower. I still did the show that night and then took myself to hospital. The doctors' annoyance at my stupidity was well-founded. They admitted me immediately and performed surgery the next morning.

I slowed down. I cut back on the politics and the committees and bureaucracies. I just wanted to act, it's what I was happiest doing. I got a new agent (former actor James Laurie) and started to do the rounds. There wasn't much for me in the subsidised theatre; to be honest it was understandable, and I wasn't that disappointed. It had become expensive and affected, exclusive—stories about privileged white people. The main stage theatre seemed moribund, all style with little substance. For all its posturing it was irrelevant to my life and the lives of the people I knew. I slept through it. I was more moved and stimulated by the work, simple and sophisticated, being done in communities and regions: actual stories of living in contemporary Australia. But I still did want to get back to the theatre. And this is where Scott Rankin and his company, Big hArt, came to my rescue. After our first collaboration there had been some workshops in Kalgoorlie, Wollongong, Wagga Wagga, Melbourne and Alice Springs. Now the company's shows were getting bigger and more ambitious, and were also attracting the attention of festival directors. We worked with all kinds of marginalised communities: young mothers, seniors, Indigenous, youth at risk, migrants and refugees, the homeless. We developed and toured high quality shows around the country.

Ngapartji Ngapartji told of the Pitjantjatjara people and

their displacement by the atomic testing at Maralinga in the 1950s. We rehearsed and reworked it over a few years and played most of the Australian festivals. We even trekked into the desert of Central Australia, to the people whose story it was. We rock 'n' rolled into town with scaffolding staging, sound and lighting equipment. We camped outside town in tents. Drop toilets, bush showers, big campfire, miner's lamps and swags. Wild horses and donkeys brayed and cantered through camp at night, flapping the tent, looking for food. Show time: The community huddled around camp fires, mangy dogs and snotty kids running around in anticipation of what was about to occur.

The choir that night included all the women, about twenty of them, who had been in the show over the past two years. When they sang the hymns and rock songs in language, the red dust of the desert stirred. The audience was laughing, cheering and crying. It felt pure and primal. It transcended time and place. Maybe I was hallucinating. Unfortunately, I had woken up with the runs and was throwing up, body aching, sweating and shivering. During the show, I dashed to the side railing and threw up into the scrub below. Then did the next scene. Then dash and throw up. Next scene. Dash and hurl. I told Scott it was a post-modern way of critiquing the show: while it was happening.

I've learned a lot from working with communities, particularly those who are socially marginalised. Often it has been with Big hArt, other times with similar companies and organisations. The stories are usually personal and relevant, seeking political and social outcomes. The performers are non-career artists and usually untrained, but there is an authenticity about these stories that is often humbling, poignant and powerful. As one of the trained performers, I relish the responsibility of sharing these stories, assisting in their theatrical development and supporting the performers, who may be understandably inconsistent and nervous. Part of my job is to help shape and drive the performance, to be constantly prepared to accommodate the unexpected. Whether raw or sophisticated, involving simple or complex ideas, these shows are fundamentally about making positive changes to the lives of people, giving them a voice in public discourse. I believe this is when theatre is at its most sublime.

The most ambitious project of all, *Hipbone Sticking Out*, which premiered as part of the Centenary of Canberra in 2013, was developed over a number of years in the magnificent Pilbara. It told the story of the region, using mythology, western classicism, music and technology, to address themes of incarceration and resilience. The Melbourne Festival season was a triumph. Artistically, emotionally, intellectually, visually, musically, theatrically. It deserved to be seen by the world. That fact it wasn't suggests something amiss with our arts funding policies.

Unfortunately, this work is often low on the priorities of the arts and cultural agencies, which distribute public funding. There is a lot to admire about the work of the Australia Council and the various state and territory bodies, but the arts, which individually pride themselves on innovation, are in public life paradoxically conservative. At the elite level we seem to value the western classical tradition and benchmark everything against it. It's where the majority of the money goes, supporting the flagship companies. And yet, it is those very companies that are best positioned to leverage sponsorship, benefaction and subscription. Public funding is a minor percentage of their annual turnover. Today, when so many arts organisations have lost funding, it is the major companies that again have been protected. The diversity of voices on the street is being lost in the theatre, for it is to the smaller companies that we look, for the new work, the innovation, the research and development.

Actors subsidise this work, receiving a pittance—a share of the box office should the production make a meagre profit. But I remember John Sumner, theatre producer of the old school, arguing for the contrary, the central importance of research and risk: Virtually anyone could mount a production of *Hamlet*, he told us; but new work required and deserved the best resources the company could provide. Apparently, funding bodies disagree.

In between Big *h*Art gigs, I did some other theatre including several independent co-ops. The extinction of small and mid-sized companies in recent times, and the amount of new work being subsidised by artists working for a cut of the door, is just one symptom of something really amiss with our arts funding. Apart from the theatre, I've had the occasional film, some radio and television.. And then, occasionally, a gift like *The Slap* comes along.

It still remains harder for actors from non-Anglo backgrounds to find employment. We still don't have the confidence to allow an organically blended cast to exist without commenting upon it. Despite initiatives to stimulate 'colour-blind casting' and the good work being done by the ABC, SBS, and some theatre companies, casting in 2017 still remains stereotypical and tokenistic; a sense of exotica, a generalised 'otherness' still prevails. I still get offers to play nationalities other than Greek. If the part is culturally-specific, I decline, with thanks. If it about more universal issues, I have a look and see if I can engage with the material.

Since I returned to being a jobbing actor, I've also completed my teaching qualifications, which enable me to work in the Vocational Education and Training (VET) sector. I enjoy the discipline of learning, the campus atmosphere, the collegiality of the staff, and above all, the chance to work with young actors and to learn from them. I harbour a guilty suspicion that I learn more than the students.

The phone still rings, albeit not as frequently as it once did, but that's fine by me and I understand. I'm not the hustler I once was. My circumstances have changed. We have a growing tribe of grandchildren, and I'm more interested in picking up babysitting gigs. The pay's not as good but the rewards are immeasurable.

5. The Actor's role

And so, it is by this circuitous route that I found myself in a gutter in Waterloo, covered in rotting tomatoes. I recalled the beautiful poem, 'Ithaka', by Greece's finest modern poet, Konstantine Kavafy. It's his advice to Herakles about the labours he faced on his long journey home. It concludes:

> *Ithaka gave you the marvellous journey.*
> *Without her you wouldn't have set out.*
> *She has nothing left to give you now.*
> *And if you find her poor, Ithaka won't have fooled you.*
> *Wise as you will have become, so full of experience,*
> *You'll have understood by then what these Ithakas mean.*

So if acting is my Ithaka, what have I learned from the journey?

For me, the salient point is the primacy of the actor's role in the creative process. To emphasise this point, Stella Adler would brandish a script as if it were the Ten Commandments, point to the actors and declaim in a stentorian tone that brooked no negotiation, 'Without YOU this is literature! Without YOU this does not live!' Most producers, directors, writers and designers understand this and value the actor's contribution. But for some, actors still remain a necessary evil. Temperamental, untrustworthy, egomaniacal children who should been seen and not heard. Needless to say, this completely blocks the creative process and inevitably leads to an inferior result.

I would like to think I have become a better storyteller, more direct and economical. Less inclined to get in the way of the story. I feel comfortable and relaxed on stage. I have consolidated my process. Basically, it's Stella Adler with some embellishments and amendments picked up along the way. Let me emphasise that all actors are different, and this is about what I do. I'm not preaching to anyone, or saying this is how it should be done. Through a process of trial and error, this is what works for me, that's all.

The script is my primary source. The first thing I do is delete all stage directions except essential physical actions. I don't want the writer telling me how to say something, that's for me to discover. If the writing is good, the emotion should be inherent in the script. Abstract adverbs like 'sadly', 'happily', 'angrily' are absolutely useless to me. I can't play a quality, I can only play an action. Did Shakespeare instruct us on how we should deliver 'To be or not to be'? 'Sadly', 'happily', 'angrily'? The American actor Christopher Walken deletes all punctuation also from his scripts, leaving only the words. And I think it shows. It's what I like about his performances: they are unpredictable, idiosyncratic, oddly punctuated.

So I read the script and react to it. First impressions of

story, possible themes, characters, dialogue, style. Using my favourite script pencil, I circle unfamiliar words, names and places. I populate the margins with question marks. 'I wonder what that means?'

Then I start my research. This is the essential foundation I need before I can attempt to tell the story. Research is my security blanket. Since my student days, I've always loved it and its importance was emphasised by Ms Adler. I look at the 'given circumstances' in the script. The time and place, the people, the events. I look at my character. What do we know about him? His age, occupation, relationship to the other characters. What does he say and do? What do others say about him and do to him?

Then I break the script down into scenes and further down to beats, small pieces of action. My questions become more speculative. Why does he say that? And do that? What does he want? How does he want to affect the other character? What is his action? At the same time I research the play and the writer, the period and place that contextualise the play. I read about the social, political, and artistic movements of the time. I look at paintings and photos for some visual clues to period and character. What music would he have listened to?

I try to achieve all this before rehearsals start. I want to concentrate on the script and allow my imagination free rein, supported by the research. Working with the director and the other actors on the journey of discovery and execution is the most exciting part of the process for me. Experimenting with different choices and actions, being receptive to what the others bring, constructing the performance, finding the rhythms, allowing the story to unfold. I seek out the new information in any scene, feeling how it advances the story. I try to experience things for the first time.

This is where grandchildren are very helpful. When I babysit I can observe their simple pleasures and hurts. Running around in the rain, on the swings, patting the dog. The purity of their response is valuable material for an actor. If only I could bottle their innocence. The English director, Jonathan Miller, once said that a big part of his job involved getting actors to forget things they should never remember, and remember things they should never forget. I try not to repeat things I have done before, it's such a lazy shortcut. I like to keep my options open as late as possible to allow for the needs of the other actors. Once a scene is working to everyone's satisfaction, I'm happy to place it on the back of the stove on a low simmer, and wait for an audience.

Once the show is on, it tends to dominate my day. Everything is timed around the curtain rising at eight o'clock. I usually have a late lunch and a light snack before the show. I don't like performing on a full stomach. I might try and have a short nap in the afternoon. I drink plenty of fluids, non-alcoholic. I check that my voice is working. I like to arrive about an hour before the curtain. Normally I don't drink coffee in the evening, but if I'm doing a show I will have one for that little caffeine hit. Once I enter the theatre, I switch off my phone and leave the events of the day behind. I start to focus on the show. I check my props and costumes, walk around the stage muttering lines to myself. I do a light vocal and physical warm-up. Once I'm satisfied everything is working I don't overdo it. I conserve energy for the show. In the dressing room there is usually some light banter, a bit of gossip maybe. Everyone is different in the way they prepare. I gradually withdraw into myself and just focus on what I need to do. I always have the script with me and like to glance at it, trying to see the words for the first time.

I'm confident enough now to allow the show to happen. I'll play my actions but the lines will be delivered differently each time. They will be an expression of how I'm feeling at that moment. Each audience is individual and so, therefore, is each show. The basic architecture will remain the same, but the interior decorating will change. Back in the dressing room, I don't analyse the scene that's just gone. That can wait until after the show. I can't change what's happened. I need to concentrate on the next scene, change costume, have a drink, recalibrate for what is to come.

When the show's over, we usually have a chat and a couple of laughs about the performance. Unless I'm meeting friends, I then toddle off home. If it's an emotionally taxing show, which forces me into uncomfortable mental spaces, I take Daisy for a late night walk. I have a smoke, watch television, read, sleep, and with luck I wake up again next morning. Then I start preparing for that night's performance. And so it goes, very enjoyable factory work.

It is somewhat different in film and television, although the basics remain the same. *Kingswood Country* was really weekly rep with the same characters. The script would arrive at the start of the week, we'd rehearse for the next few days before going to the studio. There we would rehearse with the cameras and then play in front of a live audience. After that I would have a meal and a nap before repeating the performance for a second audience. This minimised the amount of stoppages and retakes, and enabled the producers to edit between the two recordings, choosing the best scenes from each. Inevitably the first show felt like a dress rehearsal and the second show tended to provide the bulk of the final edit. Multicam studio drama is more or less the same but without an audience.

Film and miniseries are different again, and present particular acting challenges. Whereas theatre is linear and continuous, allowing the actor a logical emotional journey, film is fragmented. Murphy's Law dictates that your big scenes, often late in the narrative, will be scheduled before your establishing scenes, and these will be shot last. The actor has to be very clear about the story and where he is emotionally at any given point. Preparation is paramount.

The Slap

I had been a big fan of Christos Tsiolkas' writing since his debut novel, *Loaded*, and as soon as I read *The Slap*, and heard that it was to be adapted into a mini-series, I knew I wanted to be in it. Only problem was I wasn't sure whom I could play. I was too old for the main male characters, Hector and Harry, and seemingly too young for the father, Manolis. Nevertheless I was thrilled to get an audition. I practised my Greek and applied what I hoped was a subtle amount of makeup to seem a bit older. The audition went well and I received a call back. Again it went well, and now it was a matter of whether I could look old enough. Personally, I didn't think it was that big a stretch, but I was hardly objective. We consulted with the makeup supervisor and she confirmed that she didn't think it would be too big a problem, and so I had the green light. Next obstacle concerned my health. With a dicky ticker and leukaemia I couldn't pass the medical without indemnifying the insurers and providing guarantees from my doctors that my pre-existing conditions would not hamper my ability to work. Eventually all the hurdles were jumped, negotiations concluded and contracts signed.

I cleared all other commitments, corporate gigs, radio and teaching, so I could concentrate on the task ahead. The truth was that the leukaemia was becoming fairly enervating and I wanted to conserve as much energy as I could for what I knew would be a gruelling shoot.

I began my preparation by re-reading the novel, gathering all the information about Manolis in order to build his back story. I began my wider research using the massive archive about Greek Australians that my friends, photographer Effy Alexakis and historian Leonard Janiszewski, had accumulated. I listened tearfully to some interviews Leonard have done with Dad. I talked to Christos' father and tried to capture some of his vocal mannerisms. I looked at photos and listened to Greek music from the period. Until I felt I knew Manolis. I had grown up with men like him, and witnessed the struggles they had endured to raise families, working dirty, punishing jobs, seeking comfort and solace among their compatriots, trying to fit in, trying to educate their kids.

The story was told over eight episodes, of which one (episode six) was driven by Manolis. I extracted all his scenes from the scripts and put them together, discarding everything else so that I was just working with his story. This became my 'bible'. I wanted to remain ignorant of anything that didn't involve him. I deleted all of the scripted suggestions and worked just with his dialogue and what he did. Then I started plotting his emotional journey, his actions and discoveries, breaking them down into 'beats'.

I worked with a dialogue coach, Kosta Nikas, to try and make my Greek sound native-born rather than inflected with my Australian accent. I translated my English dialogue into Greek and learned it that way, forcing myself to think Greek and translate back into English before speaking. Externally, I let my facial hair go untrimmed, allowing it to sprout from my ears and nostrils, eyebrows running wild. I put on some kilos (without much effort), stopped taking anti-inflammatory medication, allowing the stabs of osteoarthritis to remind me of my physical (and spiritual) deterioration. To produce Manolis's limp I used an old acting trick of putting a pebble in my shoe.

Crucially for me, I used objects belonging to my father: his *komboloi* (worry beads), Hellenic Club membership badge, key ring. I wanted that connection to Dad and his generation of migrants. Indeed, that connection was reinforced during the make-up process as the ageing prosthetics were applied. I began to anticipate the moment where I could look in the mirror and no longer see myself, but my father. Even now, when I see an image for *The Slap*, I still think I'm looking at Dad.

Film and television provide minimal rehearsal time and the actor is meant to deliver on the day. I use the set-up time to try the scene a couple of ways, giving the director some choices. Once we agree on what we are doing, I try to remain engaged through multiple takes and different set-ups. I give myself tiny challenges to keep it fresh until we're done with it.

Film involves a lot of waiting around interspersed with short bouts of intense activity. I try not to use up nervous energy between scenes. I read or listen to music, have a cup of tea, a nap if time permits. Once again, I trust my preparation and only re-engage with the script and character when my next scene is called.

6. The Actor's life

As one of my colleagues is fond of saying, 'I can teach you to act, but I can't teach you how to be an actor.'

Touring

Actors have always been itinerant workers. That hasn't changed, if anything modern transport has increased our itinerancy. It's one of the things that attracted me to acting: the opportunity to experience different theatres in different towns and cities and countries. However, touring can be difficult and hazardous. The universal rule applies: what happens on tour stays on tour. What happens on tour is sometimes exhilarating, frequently hilarious, usually unhealthy, often immoral, occasionally illegal, and intermittently boring. Actors die on tour, go mad, drink too much, smoke too much, and eat poorly. Romances bloom and feuds escalate, lifelong friendships are forged, secrets are shared. You wear the same clothes, watch meaningless television, and become accustomed to soft mattresses and hard pillows. You need to be resilient.

I try to force some discipline onto the chaos. If I'm anywhere for longer than a week, I unpack the mini-bar and give it back to housekeeping, not so much to remove the temptation as to fill the fridge with fruit and food and snacks. Electronic devices ensure I have plenty of books. Otherwise I'm an excellent tourist, always happy to visit galleries and museums, join in company events or remain comfortable on my own. I have to avoid being idle, because that's when I make poor choices.

Alcohol

Grog and actors have been inseparable since they were first introduced to one another. Many an actor has been, to use John Clarke's whimsical phrase, 'a martyr to the turps'. The ancient Greek performances were in honour of the god of wine, revelry and fertility. It's safe to assume that Thespis and all the thespians after him, took their curtain call, divested themselves of robes and masks, put on a party frock and headed for the bar, eager to allow their admirers to buy drinks for them.

According to *The Australian Actors' Wellbeing Study*:

> *Actors use alcohol at levels well above the World Health Organisation guidelines for healthy consumption. Male actors consume alcohol at levels that are significantly higher than their female counterparts; however, both males and females report alcohol consumption at potentially harmful levels. This finding is consistent with actors' reports, in our survey, of their reliance on alcohol as a means with which to both 'cool down' after performance and to cope with the more acute effects of demanding roles. It also appears that much of the drinking is associated with forms of sociality linked to working in this field.*[14]

A friend, an eminent television and theatre producer/director, told me of a recent occasion when a young actress, obviously distressed, told him that she didn't 'feel safe' sharing a scene with a certain actor, she was afraid he was drunk. My friend acted swiftly and confronted the young man, who said he was just acting drunk, exploring the character. Peace and safety were restored and the scene was shot. My friend had acted responsibly and appropriately. However, he later confessed that he had not been as truthful as he might have: he should have advised the young woman that if she wanted a career, she must learn how to work with drunks.

I admit to performing drunk a couple of times in my early days, indeed in one theatre-restaurant show in Sydney in the 1970s the whole cast was pissed. But I didn't enjoy it. I felt guilty that I had let people down, especially the audience. I don't like working with drunks—they are slow, lines get lost, props are fumbled, scenes lose rhythm and shape, the story becomes fragmented and obscure. Meaning is a casualty. I would like to think we could achieve a paradigm shift if we provided young actors with resilience training, but I'm sceptical.

Of course, many actors don't drink and many others drink responsibly and moderately. Needless to say, there are lots of funny stories about drunken actors. My favourite concerns the English actor Wilfred Lawson, who turned up for a matinee performance and sat in the audience. At a certain point he nudged the person beside him and declared joyously, 'This is where I come on.' God love him, he was there to watch himself. An existential scene worthy of Beckett.

Drugs

The Australian Actors' Wellbeing Study also reported that:

> *about 80 per cent of the actors in this study are active users of either legal or illegal drugs [...] This suggests, perhaps, that actors actively self-medicate in response to both the general, long-term pressures of their work and lives, and the acute burdens of demanding roles.*[15]

And then there's the recreational use of drugs. I confess to being a user, part of the 80 per cent, and once performed stoned. It was frightening. I was loud and slow and paranoid. I hated being out of control. I never did it again. But once the show is over, that's another matter. I don't care what anybody does in the privacy of their own home, so long as they hurt no one and show up fit to work the next day. Too many actors have developed fatal addictions, some have overdosed, and others have had psychotic episodes and/or developed mental disorders that left them incapable of working. The most horrendous case I can recall concerned a handsome, young leading man, who, at the height of the psychedelic era had a particularly bad acid trip, during which he chopped off his own foot. Then there was the despicable film director who encouraged his actors to try heroin so they could be more authentic in their roles. This led to a fourteen-year addiction for one of my friends.

Drugs highlight one of the great paradoxes of our business. Actors are encouraged and rewarded for taking artistic risks. We love actors who bring a touch of danger to their work. Stella Adler summed it up when she stated: 'Actors need a kind of aggression, a kind of inner force. Don't be only one-sided—sweet, nice, good. Get rid of being average. Find the killer in you.'[16] But is it reasonable to expect risk-taking to have an on/off switch and not infiltrate our personal life?

When I was young and touring, the first thing I packed was my drugs. Now, it's my medication. *Plus ça change, plus c'est la même chose.* I remember one incident fondly. It was in Melbourne at the APG in the 1970s. The members of the collective belonged to one of two groups, the drinkers and the smokers, although many held dual membership. There was a sub-group of heroin users who kept pilfering the kitchen spoons whenever they needed a fix. The collective was annoyed at this drain on resources and came up with the solution: they drilled a hole in each of them.

Health

Both physical and mental health are a major concern for the jobbing actor, since our body, voice and mind are our tools of trade and we need to keep them in good order. The show must go on, and it does. In the commercial theatre there are understudies, but no such luxury exists in the non-commercial theatre. If an actor can't perform, then a replacement is quickly found even if it means performing book-in-hand. Audiences are usually understanding and generous. What to you and me is a common cold is a loss of earnings for a voice/over artist. Back pain can end a dancer's career. Singers lose their voice and along with it their livelihood. Actors above all must have stamina and a high threshold for pain. I've performed variously with broken bones, inflamed vertebra, nosebleeds, influenza, depression, dysentery, nausea, and leukaemia. Once in Canberra I contracted Bell's palsy, which made one side of my face numb and drooping. (I maintained the palsy had hung around after a season by the Bell Shakespeare Co., and I had caught it when I warmed up with 'To be or not to be.') I slurred and dribbled my way through the show like a drunk.

The only performance I've missed was in Perth when I had the heart attack. I was back the next night with two stents and a comfy chair. The show must go on. I'm not touting for your sympathy. I mention it because most actors after a number of years would boast a similar medical history. I've seen actors collapse, vomit, shit themselves, piss themselves, and still complete the show. It's not uncommon for actors to die on, or just off, stage, on a film set or in a television studio. If that sounds unlikely, put 'actors die on stage' into your search engine and marvel at the results.[17] Stage combat, physical scenes, stunts, hazardous sets and inappropriate costumes can all lead to physical injury, no matter how safely they may have been choreographed or constructed. Incidentally, there are not many things funnier than seeing a dancer pull a hamstring. I know I shouldn't laugh, but I defy anyone not to.

More alarming are the mental health issues that bedevil actors. Another recent survey discovered that performers experience depression five times higher than the general population; moderate-severe anxiety ten times higher;

suicide twice as much; suicide ideation 5–7 times higher; sleep disorders seven times greater.[17]

I'm disturbed by the number of students I meet who are on anti-depressants or similar treatment for mental disorders. I can understand it to an extent. Today they come into a world rife with war, terrorism, tyranny, unemployment, poverty, injustice, climate change and social media. A more unstable world than the one in which I grew up. And then they choose a profession that exacerbates those feelings of instability within an industry that contains, the survey notes, 'a powerful, negative culture [...] including a toxic, bruising work environment; extreme competition; bullying; sexual assault; sexism and racism.' If they can gain employment, most (63%) will earn less than the Australian National Minimum Wage of $34,112.[18]

I don't have figures for the incidence of sexually-transmitted diseases, but would confidently wager that it is also several times higher than the national average. We should pause to remember the generation that was decimated by the AIDS epidemic of the 1980s and 90s. The Grim Reaper blighted all levels of society, but he stayed too long in showbiz.

So what can be done? Resilience training is becoming more acknowledged as a necessary component of actor training. For the ability to identify stress and anxiety, and to help creative artists manage the impact of these conditions, this knowledge is vitally important. Various exercises and practices are being formulated for groups and/or individuals to enable them to create a healthier work environment. We must become better at it and more diligent as we mentor and inform our heirs, the new links in our chain. The larger companies are starting to demonstrate an awareness of it at an administrative level, and this needs to infiltrate the organisation. The large subsidised companies must be encouraged to provide resilience skills and counselling to the actors they employ. The smaller, independent companies will have to do whatever they can without resources.

Family

Having a supportive family is crucial to an actor's health— at least it is to mine. And I've been blessed. My wife Anne trained and worked in the business and understands the demands and vagaries of being an actor. Weird hours, fragile egos, moods, obsessive behaviour, the stench of disappointment, the rush of success, not much money. Actors are not easy to live with, and I think it is sometimes confronting for non-acting partners. My family provides me with stability, gives my life a purpose, and keeps me involved in the 'real' world. They are also the source of deep emotional experiences, which enrich me and, by extension, influence my work.

Dogs

My family has always had them and they contribute greatly to my sense of wellbeing. They take me for a walk and unconditionally love me. No matter what sort of crappy day I might have had or how anxious I may be feeling, it's great to have someone who is pleased to see me, who wags their tail and licks my face. It's too easy for actors to become completely self-absorbed, and I think the responsibility of caring for someone else is healthy. Our dogs have been great companions as we walk; and I learn lines, or voice my thoughts, vent my spleen. When I was preparing for *The Slap* I needed to revive my Greek and took to practising it with the dog. At that time, it was a lovely little fellow, Joey. Part fox terrier, part bull terrier, part mountain goat. Initially he was confused. By the time we'd finished shooting he was bilingual in all his basic commands, and some conversation. He even began eating squid. I'm trying to go further with our current dog, Daisy the greyhound. I'm teaching her French as well.

7. The Actor at work

The Director

The relationship between actor and director is crucial in the development of a production. The director usually has a vision of what he/she wants it to be. The actor collaborates through discussion and experimentation in order to realise that vision. Acting is an act of faith. You can't do it and watch it at the same time, so I need the director to tell me whether what I think I'm doing is what he/she is seeing. Is the story clear? Am I telling it well? How can I make it better? Are we all in the same play? The director is your first audience and shapes what the real audience will receive. There is no performance without an audience, and ultimately the audience are the ones who tell the actor what works and what doesn't. An invisible, umbilical cord is established, a contract is entered into, as actor and audience react to one another.

The challenge for the director is to unite a cast. Of course, some companies are identified with a certain style and methodology and this makes it easier. But more often it is an ad hoc cast, each of whom has their own process, and it is up to the director to make them a team. Some will start externally and work their way into the character, others may start internally and allow the externals to

be added later. Some get there quickly and the director's challenge may be to slow them down, create some
diversions before they freeze their performance. Others
may painstakingly struggle at first before bringing it all
together. The director needs to deal with all of this and
ensure everyone is in readiness by the time the audience
arrives. As an actor, I need to be open to accommodating
the working idiosyncrasies of other actors. I'm always
interested in seeing how other actors solve problems and
I learn from their approach. I'm delighted and a little
envious when I see an actor solve a problem in a way
that I would never have considered. Equally, I'm puzzled
when I see an actor struggling with an issue, which to me,
seems so simple. My own process is always, consciously
and unconsciously, influenced by those with whom I'm
working. All directors have their own individual process
and I have learned from each of them. Different ways to
approach the text and actors, different rehearsal drills and
procedures. Sad to say, there are still some directors who
don't really understand actors and instead are autocratic.
This manner rarely fails to make the project less successful
than it otherwise might have been.

The Writer

Working with writers is different again. But in the theatre
the opportunity doesn't occur that often. Imagine having
Shakespeare in the room while rehearsing *Hamlet*. 'So,
Will, 'to be or not to be', what's that about? I'm not sure
that at this point in the play I should be thinking about
suicide. It just seems a bit clumsy and overwritten.' But

we must respect the writer. To corrupt Ms Adler's exhortation, 'without *them*, you don't have a gig!' In rehearsal conditions, if the writer is there (and there is usually only one) they are the most vulnerable person in the room. For a new writer it can be overwhelming. My obligation is to respect what they've written and try to show it to them before entering into discussion. Often writers will discover things that they hadn't considered or articulated. Some scenes may be cut and replaced by new ones. Some sections will be overwritten and others need more. Not all actors are comfortable working on a new script, but I love it. I relish the forensic dramaturgy that is needed to excavate a script and present the writer's intentions.

Of course, in film and television, an actor is working with new scripts all the time, and the distinctive nature of the medium requires a different kind of dramaturgy, one which considers what the camera will see, and how variously the story can be told. I noticed as a film director that one of the differences between really good film actors and not so good ones, was their attitude to the script. The not-so-good ones always had some extra lines they would like to add, to puff their character a bit. These were easily dismissed. The good actors chose the reverse. They had suggestions about what they could cut, confident that they could tell the story better and more economically. Usually they were right.

As far as voice-over in radio is concerned, presentation and narration scripts make different demands on actors with vocal skills: most importantly, the ability to sight read. It's an underrated skill, one that can be learned and mastered. I've been surprised at the number of actors

who have some form of dyslexia—actors of my generation who were bullied and told they were stupid because
they couldn't read or write well. In some cases, it was the
motivating reason they became actors.

The Designer

Actors should also collaborate with the designers. Sets that
look fabulous are often hazards that are perilous to negoti-
ate in the dark. Actors have the right to a safe work place.
There was a time when raked stages were all the rage, and
the angles were getting steeper and steeper. Actors were
developing chronic back, hip and knee conditions. Now
there is a maximum gradient allowed for raked stages.
But the relationship with the set cannot be all adversarial.
Designers bring superb vision to a play and actors should
be enabled to learn the set well in advance of performance,
and how best to utilise it to make their statement.

Costume designers are different again and their relationship with the actor is a more direct one. They provide a
visual representation of the character and this can be really
useful, showing a way of seeing the character. Sometimes
it can be disarming if it's not how you were thinking of the
character. Other times it can stop character development
in its tracks. So costume designers should meet early with
the actors. There is usually some room for negotiation, but
in the larger companies production schedules demand that
design decisions are finalised and costumes made before
rehearsals begin. In that case all you can do is nod and
appreciate the costume design as a fine piece of drawing
and colouring in. One designer used to make me laugh

with his single-mindedness. His costume sketches were always of someone slender and as tall as an AFL full forward, even when he knew it was I playing the role. I kept reminding him that the costume would not look like that on me but he stuck to his vision. Actors should also be wary of costumes that are impractical and limit what you need to do physically in the play. Comfort is an only-occasional luxury. Best to assume that if the costume is uncomfortable it must look good. Either that, or the designer hates you.

The Crew

And finally, in the creative process, actors need to love and respect the crew. Stage managers, operators, front of house, dressers, mechs and techs. Without them, you don't have a show. Be particularly nice to the mechanists. They're the ones in charge of the sandbags and they can be dropped from a great height. Sometimes an unpopular actor can be standing underneath.

8. New links in the chain

This year another three hundred actors will graduate from public and private training colleges around the country. They will be better trained than actors ever have been. Apart from their acting skills, they will have also been trained in marketing and technology, financial planning and legal requirements, lifestyle and resilience skills. They will have a show reel, a voice tape and a five-year plan. Bubbling with enthusiasm, ambition and apprehension, they will try to find an agent and a job. They will shoot and edit their own auditions and screen tests at home before sending them off to producers. Some will be lured to try their luck in London, Los Angeles or New York, while others will pursue further study. Some may drift into different artistic disciplines, while others may decide it's not for them and seek more regular employment. All will have just a year to establish themselves before the marketplace receives the next three hundred graduates.

All of them will aspire to find a place in the grand tradition of storytelling that stretches back to the camp fire and the cave. And for all the study they have done, they will still learn the most from those who have been before them. Above all else, acting is an oral tradition with the tricks of the trade passing from one generation to the next. This was beautifully articulated by the soprano,

Emma Matthews, who recently played Nellie Melba in a new Australian musical:

> *My teacher's teacher's teacher's teacher was Nellie Melba. So I have developed my career on the same vocal technique that she was taught by Madame [Mathilde] Marchesi. Now I'm teaching my students the same technique. It is a lineage that has come to me.*[20]

I would like to conclude with two quotations that have stood me in good stead all my working life. The first is from Chekhov's *The Seagull*. Nina, the young actress, has returned after a disastrous affair with an older writer, and the death of her child. She tells her friend (who has always been in love with her) about her experience in a mediocre company:

> *I soon grew petty and dull, my acting was shallow. I didn't know what to do with my hands, I couldn't stand properly or control my voice. You can't imagine what it's like to know how badly you are acting. [...] I'm no longer like that. Now I am a real actress. I act with joy, with rapture, I am intoxicated by it, and feel that I am really good. [...] Now I know, finally I understand, that for us, whether it's acting or writing, it is not the fame and fortune that I once dreamt of that matters, it is the ability to endure. To bear one's cross, and believe. I have belief, and so don't suffer so much, and when I think of my vocation, I'm not afraid of life.* (adapted by Lex Marinos)

The ability to endure. The need to believe that what you are doing is worthwhile. The apprehension that the job transcends skill and talent, handy as those things are. As every year passes this passage becomes more reverberant for me. However, every time I read it, another little voice in my brain urges me to remember Katharine Hepburn, remember Katharine Hepburn. And I do. The great lady once said:

> *Acting is the most minor of gifts and not a very high-class way to earn a living. After all, Shirley Temple could do it at the age of four.*

Most days I oscillate between the twin peaks of Nina and Kate. I like my idealism to be tempered by common sense. I want my feet to be on the ground while my head is in the clouds.

See you in the dark. Tomatoes optional.

Endnotes

1 George Sorlie (1883–1945) was a West Indian performer whose tent show with his wife Grace Stewart toured NSW and Queensland 1917–45 playing melodrama and pantomime and later vaudeville. After George's death the show was purchased by the comedian and dancer Bobby Le Brun, who toured it as Sorlie's Revue Company until 1961.

2 The Young Elizabethan Players were set up by the Australian Elizabethan Theatre Trust in 1958 to take abridged Shakespeare and other plays to schools under the banner, 'Shakespeare in Jeans'. Many NIDA graduates through the 1960s began their careers in this company.

3 *Saved* (1965) by Edward Bond, one of the leaders in Britain's post-war 'angry' theatre, was a principal in the successful fight for the abolition of theatre censorship. It contains a scene in which a street gang stones a baby to death in a carriage pushed by the mother.

4 Another initiative at that time, set up to attract tax deductible donations to support drama and acting students.

5 Old Tote Theatre was the name given to a small professional theatre set up on the campus of the University of
NSW in 1962 for graduating NIDA students. Its home
was the converted totalizator of the old Randwick race-
course on which the university had been built. In 1969
the Old Tote Theatre Company was chosen to develop the
official state company under the new Australia Council;
but closed in 1978 when its funding was withdrawn, and
was replaced by the Sydney Theatre Company. The Old
Tote building survives as the Figtree Theatre.

6 *The Legend of King O'Malley* (1970), by Michael Boddy
and Bob Ellis, was a pantomime created for the students
of an experimental third-year course at NIDA. It hit the
larrikin mood of the times and was taken on a national
tour. Two years later David Williamson's *Don's Party* had
a similar landmark success at Jane Street,

7 The Australian Film Development Corporation was
established in 1970; replaced by the Australian Film
Commission in 1975. The Australian Film, Television
and Radio School was established in the same period.

8 Traditional Yiddish theatre played in the world's major
cities from the nineteenth century, performing operetta.
broad comedy, satire and melodrama in the vernacular
language of the Ashkenazi. The tradition was broken by
WW2, after which the Jewish cultural styles opened to
other influences. In Stella Adler's time there would have
been up to 20 Yiddish theatres operating in the Jewish
district of New York.

9 See *A Raffish Experiment—The Selected Writings of Rex Cramphorn*. Currency Press 2009.

10 Stables Theatre, 10 Nimrod Street, Kings Cross, initially the Nimrod Street Theatre, opened in 1970, and is today the SBW Griffin Theatre.

11 Bob Ellis (1942–2016), writer, commentator and theatre enthusiast, was co-author of *The Legend of King O'Malley* and author of other works. He was a well-known figure in Sydney, known for his extravagant speeches, good intentions and disorderly dress.

12 The King O'Malley Theatre Company was so called because of the recent success of *The Legend of King O'Malley*, of which Bob Ellis had been co-writer.

13 Scott Rankin was co-founder in 1992 with John Bakes of Big *h*Art. an art and social justice production company, based in Tasmania, It works to build communities by helping the people to tell their own stories. Of their many projects the best known are *Ngapartji Ngapartji* (2004–09) and *Namatjira* (2009–present).

14 Ian Maxwell, Mark Seton and Marianna Szabó, *The Australian Actors' Wellbeing Study: A Preliminary Report*. The Equity Foundation [Actors Equity's professional development arm] in conjunction with the University of Sydney 2016.

15 *Wellbeing Study*, p.50.

16 Howard Kissel (ed.), Stella Adler, The Art of Acting. New York: Applause Books 2000.

17 https://en.wikipedia.org/wiki/List_of_entertainers_who_died_during_a_performance

18 Dr J. van den Eynde, Prof. A. Fisher, Assoc. Prof C. Sonn, *Working in the Australian Entertainment Industry*, key findings. Entertainment Assist in association with Victoria University, October 2016.

19 *Working in the Australian Entertainment Industry*, source of average wage.

20 Emma Matthews, quoted in Elissa Blake, *Sydney Morning Herald*, 10 May 2017.

COPYRIGHT
INFORMATION

PLATFORM PAPERS
Quarterly essays from Currency House Inc.
Founding Editor: Dr John Golder
Editor: Katharine Brisbane
Currency House Inc. is a non-profit association and resource centre advocating the role of the performing arts in public life by research, debate and publication.

Postal address: PO Box 2270, Strawberry Hills, NSW 2012, Australia
Email: info@currencyhouse.org.au Tel: (02) 9319 4953
Website: www.currencyhouse.org.au Fax: (02) 9319 3649

Editorial Committee: Katharine Brisbane AM, Michael Campbell, Dr Robin Derricourt, Professor Julian Meyrick, Martin Portus, Dr Nick Shimmin, Greig Tillotson

THE JOBBING ACTOR: *Rules of Engagement* © Lex Marinos 2017

ISBN 978-0-9946130-6-6
ISSN 1449-583X

Author's photograph by Greer Versteeg

Typeset in Garamond
Printed by McPherson's Printing Group

Production by XOU Creative

FORTHCOMING

PP No.54, February 2018

YOUNG PEOPLE AND THE ARTS:
An agenda for change

Sue Giles

Expectations around theatre for young people are too prescribed today, writes Sue Giles, Director of Melbourne's Polyglot Theatre. It is beset with barriers to exploration and risk-taking. Adults have long-held views on what works are appropriate and yet among all this concern for young people's creativity it is not acknowledged as art. Among those who work in the sector, the word 'value' is clouded by precedent: we struggle to be heard. In a startling expose of a system in serious need of reconstruction, Giles calls for a review of the accepted attitudes, and the embrace of a different paradigm that places children and young people at the centre of change. We must un-learn the past hierarchies, empower the engagement of children as a legitimate collaboration: valid, responsive and aware. We must recognise the power of instinctive play and imagination as intelligent modes of exploration.

AT YOUR LOCAL BOOSHOP FROM 1 FEBRUARY
AND AS A PAPERBACK OR ONLINE
FROM OUR WEBSITE AT
WWW.CURRENCYHOUSE.ORG.AU